ERIC BAUMGARTNER'S

JAZZ IT·UP!
SERIES

MID-INTERMEDIATE PIANO SOLO

FAMILIAR FAVORITES

T0081851

ISBN 978-1-4234-3626-3

EXCLUSIVELY DISTRIBUTED BY

WILLIS MUSIC

HAL•LEONARD®
CORPORATION
7777 W. BLUEMOUND RD. P.O. BOX 13819
MILWAUKEE, WISCONSIN 53213

Visit Hal Leonard Online at
www.halleonard.com

When the Saints Go Marching In

Words by Katherine E. Purvis
Music by James M. Black
Arranged by Eric Baumgartner

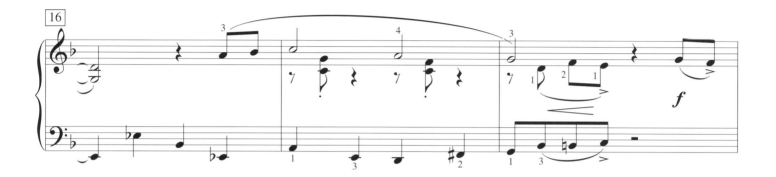

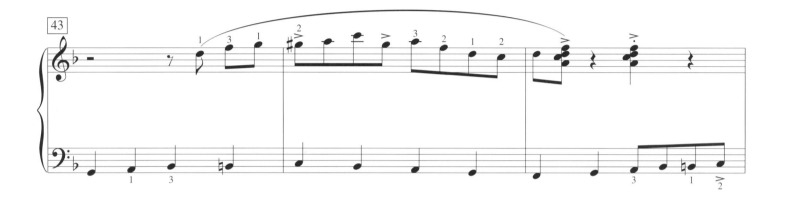

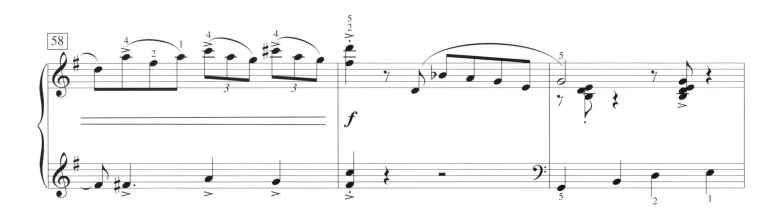

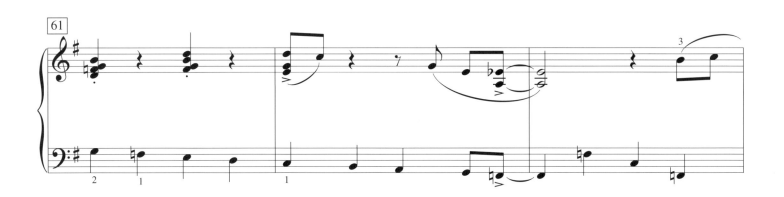

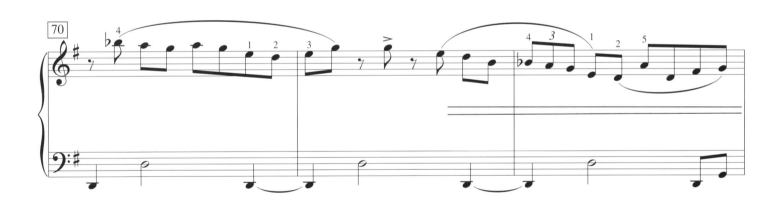

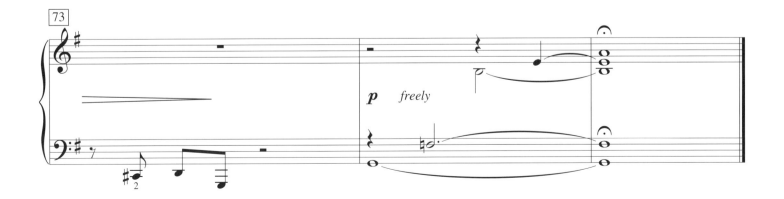

The Erie Canal

Traditional New York Work Song
Arranged by Eric Baumgartner

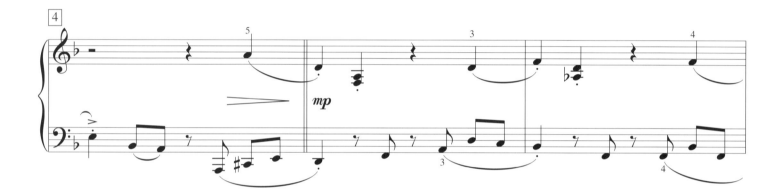

D.S. al Coda

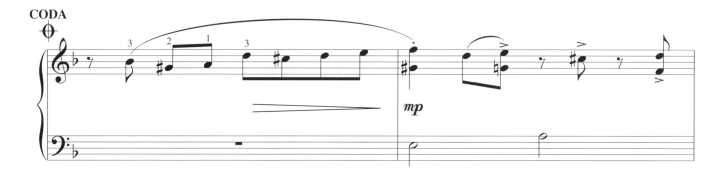

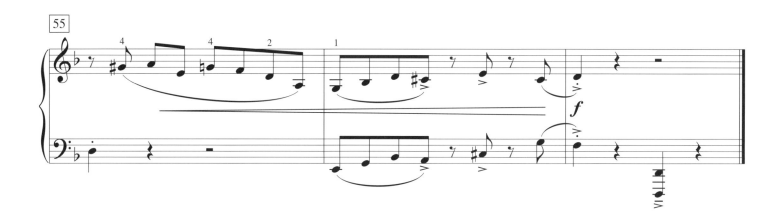

Londonderry Air
(Danny Boy)

Traditional Irish
Arranged by Eric Baumgartner

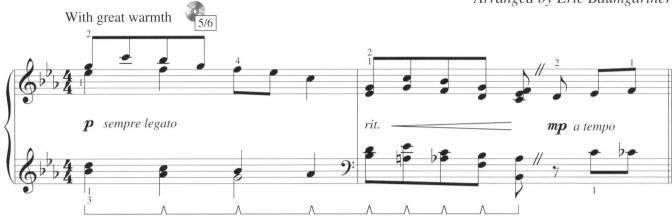

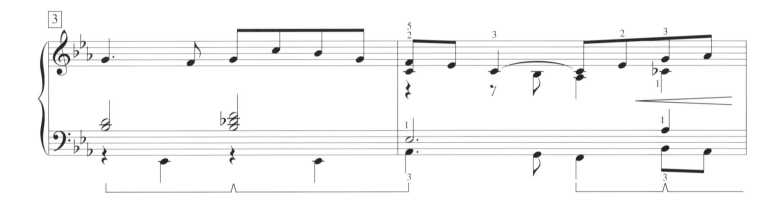

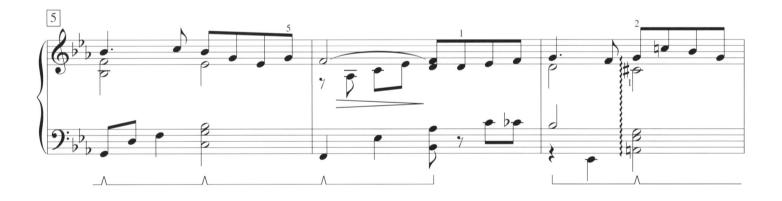

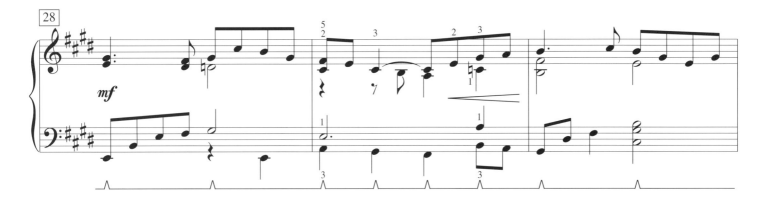

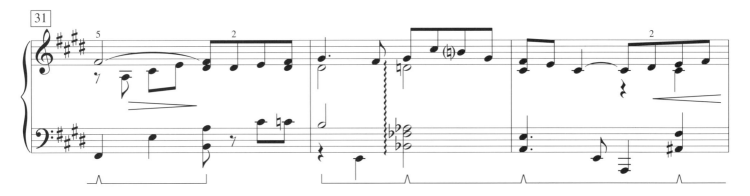

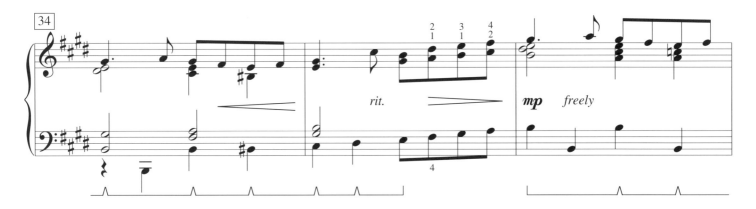

La Cucaracha

Mexican Revolutionary Folksong
Arranged by Eric Baumgartner

16

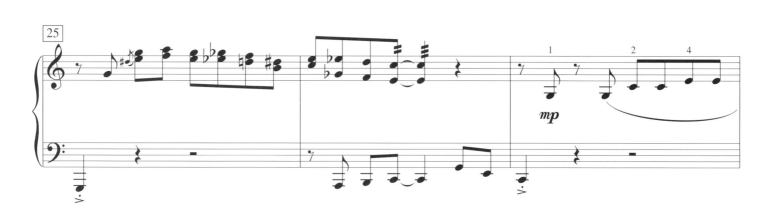

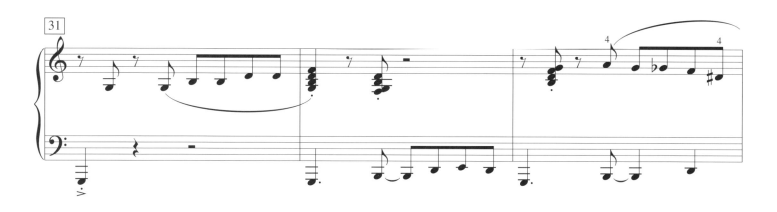

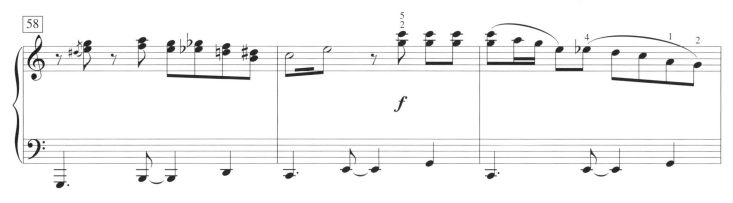

Greensleeves

16th Century Traditional English
Arranged by Eric Baumgartner

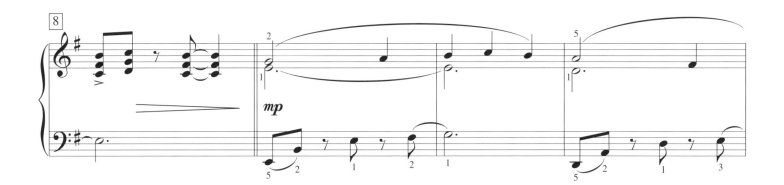

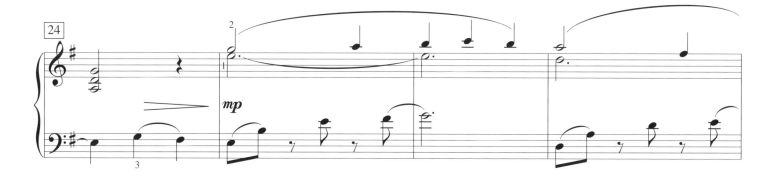

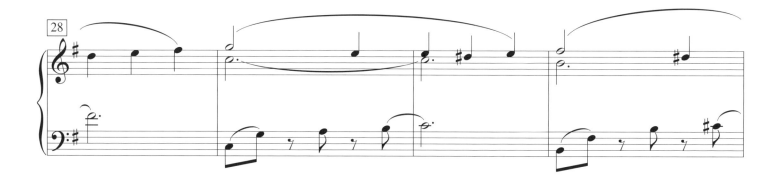

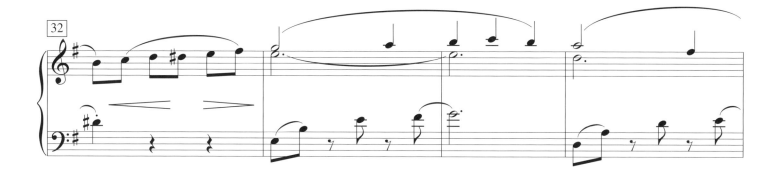

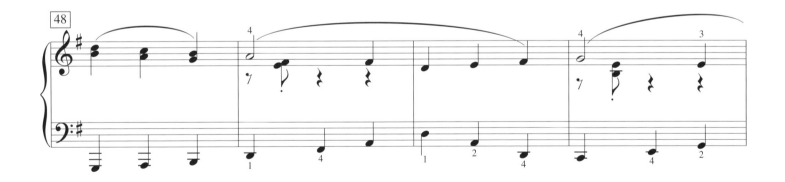

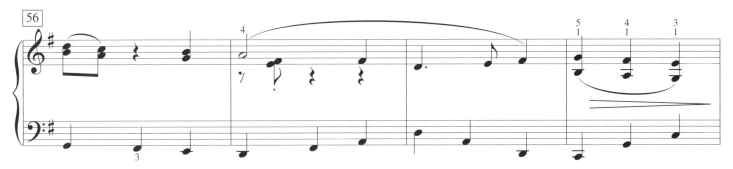

24

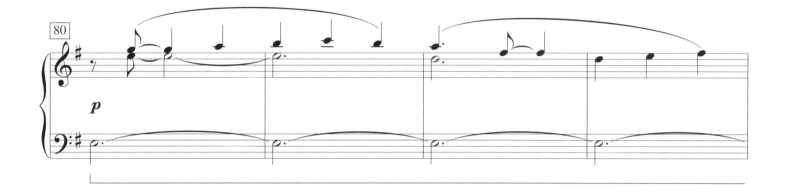

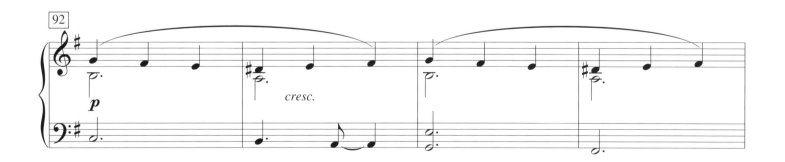

All Through the Night

Welsh Folksong
Arranged by Eric Baumgartner

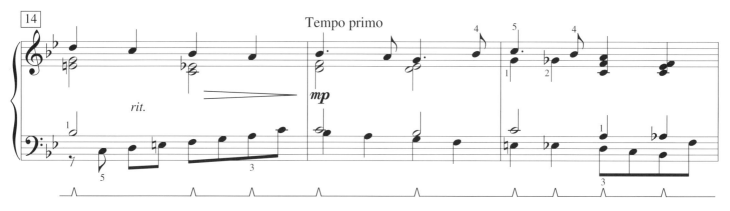

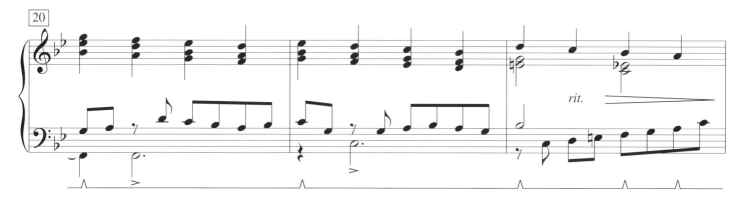

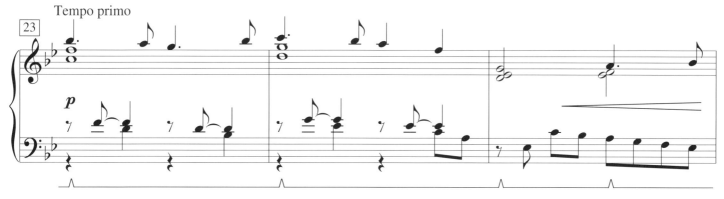

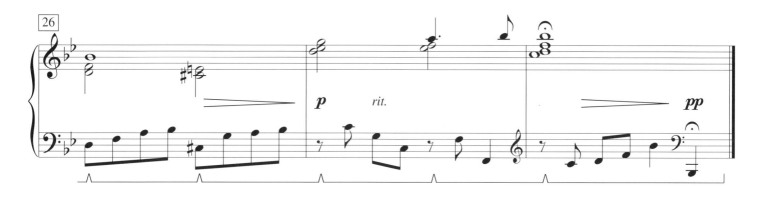

Scarborough Fair

Traditional English
Arranged by Eric Baumgartner

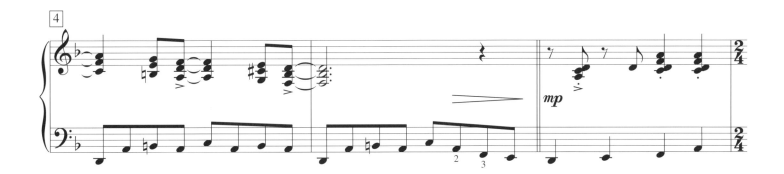

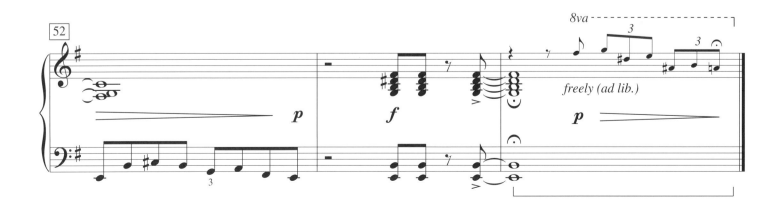

JAZZABILITIES AND JAZZ CONNECTION BOOKS
from Eric Baumgartner

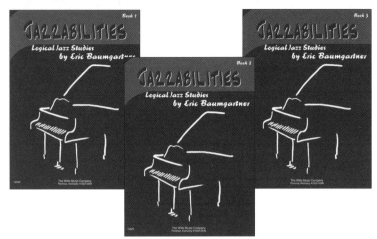

JAZZABILITIES SERIES

The **Jazzabilities** series introduces the student to the sounds of jazz through short exercises and performance pieces. The emphasis is on developing rhythmic control through jazzy melodic and harmonic bits – in essence, building a jazz vocabulary. The optional GM Disk or CD accompaniments are a great way to build rhythmic control and develop performance skills. The key to any successful performance is rhythmic control. **Jazzabilities** helps develop this control by isolating and mastering short rhythmic patterns before playing them. Basic improvisation is also introduced in this series. Each **Jazzabilities** book has a corresponding repertoire book called **Jazz Connection**. The three **Jazz Connection** books reinforce the concepts learned in **Jazzabilities** through entertaining performance pieces in a variety of jazz styles.

JAZZABILITIES, BOOK 1
Later Elementary Level
Many beginning jazz method or repertoire books are designed for the more experienced student. Book 1 is written for the later elementary level student. It uses rhythmic durations and hand positions consistent with most level 2 method books. Swing eighths and bluesy accidentals are used throughout.
00406699 Book only $6.95
00406830 Book/CD $16.95
00406832 CD only...$9.95
00406829 Book/GM Disk $16.95
00406831 GM Disk only $9.95

JAZZABILITIES, BOOK 2
Later Elementary Level
Book 2 expands on the swing rhythms and patterns learned in Book 1, while introducing the triplet and basic blues theory.
00406784 Book only...$6.95
00406835 Book/CD $16.95
00406834 Book/GM Disk $16.90

JAZZABILITIES, BOOK 3
Early Intermediate Level
The rhythmic, melodic, and harmonic vocabulary learned in the series are reinforced in Book 3, preparing the student for more advanced study in jazz theory and repertoire.
00406786 Book only $6.95
00416451 Book/CD $16.95
00416432 Book/GM Disk $16.95

JAZZ CONNECTION SERIES

Enter the stimulating world of jazz! Like its companion series **Jazzabilities**, the original performance solos in the three **Jazz Connection** books incorporate musical styles from around the globe, including rock and roll, the blues, calypso, and various Latin American beats. All the pieces in the **Jazz Connection** books were written to correspond directly with the **Jazzabilities** series, allowing the student to immediately put into play the techniques and rhythms learned in each lesson. Excellent optional accompaniments are available on CD and GM disk that will help build rhythmic control and enliven any practice session. Highly recommended for students young and old!

JAZZ CONNECTION, BOOK 1
Includes nine performance pieces
for the Later Elementary Level
00406702 Book only $5.95
00406839 Book/CD $15.95
00406845 CD only...$9.95
00406838 Book/GM Disk $15.95
00406844 GM Disk only $9.95

JAZZ CONNECTION, BOOK 2
Includes eight performance pieces
for the Later Elementary Level
00406704 Book only $5.95
00406847 Book/CD $15.95
00406846 Book/GM Disk $15.95

JAZZ CONNECTION, BOOK 3
Includes seven performance pieces
for the Early Intermediate Level
00406787 Book only $5.95
00416463 Book/CD $15.90
00416464 Book/GM Disk $15.95
00416466 GM Disk only $9.95

WILLIS MUSIC

FOR MORE INFORMATION, SEE YOUR LOCAL MUSIC DEALER,
OR WRITE TO:

HAL•LEONARD®
CORPORATION
7777 W. BLUEMOUND RD. P.O. BOX 13819 MILWAUKEE, WI 53213

0807